DON'T BURN THE UNDERWEAR

DON'T BURN THE UNDERWEAR

Susan Saper Galamba

Copyright © 2012 Susan Saper Galamba

Cover design by Carrie Kabak
www.carriekabak.com/graphics

ISBN-13: 978-1475122459 (CreateSpace-Assigned)
ISBN-10: 1475122454

For everyone contemplating or going through divorce

If reading the whole book seems too much of an undertaking right now, the author offers invaluable information in the following outline of her chapters:

Chapter 5
What information is important, and how and when should I get it?

- Attempt to voluntarily exchange documents
- Send out formal discovery if you can't get documents voluntarily, but make sure the process doesn't cost more than the information is worth
- Understand what you are looking for, why you are looking for it, and if it will make a difference in your divorce
- Pull together the last five years of tax returns
- Collect documents that evidence your incomes, assets, and debts for the last three to five years
- Assemble documentation of property and debts owned prior to the marriage
- Locate documentation of property acquired through gifts or inheritance
- Keep documents in a safe place

Chapter 6 *25*
What will happen during the divorce process, and how much will it cost?

- Know that you don't have to "serve" your spouse the divorce papers
- Understand that the cost of divorce is financial as well as emotional
- Learn that the more you communicate with your spouse, the less you'll spend in attorney's fees
- Make decisions in your divorce as you would make in business
- Check alternative dispute resolution options
- Don't leave it up to the judge

Chapter One

HOW DID I GET HERE?

It might have been you, or it might have been your spouse. Regardless of who first admitted they were unhappy, your marriage is certainly not what you imagined. However, your vows were for better or worse, and as you travel through what now feels like the "worst" part of your marriage, you figure that this too shall pass. The problem is that it rarely does. When so much is going on in your life, it's way too easy to pull the blinds on your relationship.

This all-too-common occurrence was exemplified during one of my consultations with a very attractive woman in her late thirties. She was meeting with me because her husband had just announced he was no longer in love with her and wanted a divorce. Although my client didn't doubt his words, she was still in shock. She knew things had been tough lately; however, she obviously didn't realize how bad things had gotten. She truly believed her husband's work and all the responsibilities associated with being a parent of three children meant he was just going through a difficult time. So, instead of really listening to her husband, my client's response was more: "Okay, great. Now could you please pass the mashed potatoes?"

In hindsight, she realized she should have taken his comments more seriously, but then again, it's easy to Monday morning quarterback. So, the question became not so much about how she should have reacted to her husband's comment, but rather, how did they get there in the first place?

The beginning of a relationship is easy. Craving each other's company, you'll want to spend as much time with the other person as you can, and will even talk on the phone or text until the wee hours of the morning. During this period everything is still brand new, and it's just about the two of you. Although it would be nice if relationships could stay this way, the reality is that they don't. Life is bound to start knocking at the door sooner rather than later, and you quickly find that you can go for days without having any substantive communication.

Initially your lack of communication is a result of your work schedule, because while you have already "proven" yourself at home, you still have to prove yourself at work. Whether due to traveling or working long hours, the amount of time you and your spouse have left to spend together has been significantly reduced. Frankly, even if time allowed you to talk into the wee hours of the morning, you are too tired to exert the energy.

On top of all that, throw in starting a family. As infants, children monopolize every waking hour, and as they grow your service is required as a chef, taxicab, coach, cheerleader, teacher, and consoler. By the time they are teenagers your presence is generally not required, but make no mistake about it, you need to be around. Although children are a true blessing, being a parent is the hardest and most exhausting job in the world.

While raising your children, you are like two ships passing in the night, only docking when you are presented with problems your offspring might have at school, in sports, or with friends. In short, you have to deal with issues, which certainly don't lend themselves to lighthearted or enjoyable conversations. You will either disagree on how to handle the situations, or have no time to tackle them at all. Either way **you've stopped communicating**.

To make life even more difficult, today's focus is more on children than on marriage; whereas I grew up in an era when children were to be seen and not heard. Parents participated in social events that had nothing to do with their children. However, in today's world parents' lives are completely integrated with their children's activities. If not attending a sporting event they are attending a fundraiser for the children's school.

I had a client who, married for over twenty years, had a son who was ready to graduate high school and start college. As she thought about how she and her husband were going to spend their lives as empty nesters, he was actually preparing for divorce. During our many conversations, she told me she anticipated the coming year was going to be tough because she had never spent a night away from her son since his birth, but she didn't expect to be faced with the hurdle of divorce as well.

My immediate response was, "You *never* spent a night away from your son?" When she confirmed she really meant never, I asked her if she realized that this could be part of the reason she was now sitting in my office.

There may be one in a gazillion marriages where only one spouse is at fault, but in reality, it generally takes two. **If you fail to make your marriage a priority, you may find yourself spending**

your golden years with only your children, talking about the sporting events you attended when they were younger.

As if making the children the center of attention isn't enough, you might also have to cope with aging parents, which is just the icing on the cake. It's at this point when your spouse tells you he or she isn't happy you can only respond with, "Get in line, and pass the potatoes."

Chapter Two

CAN I SAVE MY MARRIAGE?

I'm a big believer in never having any regrets. I also know marriage is not for the fainthearted, and that contemplating divorce at one time or another is normal.

It is not uncommon for clients to meet with me multiple times as they try to figure out what to do, or to meet with me on an annual basis to discuss what, if anything has changed. Some clients even file for divorce, dismiss it, and re-file only months later. Why do they do this? The answer is pretty simple—the decision to file for divorce is hard, and whoever takes the first step will inevitably spend a significant amount of time contemplating the pros and cons.

What people don't realize is that just because they are contemplating divorce doesn't mean they have to actually go through with it. If you are having doubts, the fact that an action for divorce has already been filed should not stop you from trying to save your marriage. I don't know a judge on the bench who wouldn't be thrilled to grant a couple the time they need to try and rescue their relationship. If both spouses are having second thoughts about whether divorce is the right path to take, they have every right to try and sort things out. However, the caveat to this is that *both* spouses must be equally dedicated to saving the relationship. It took two of you to get to the place you are now, and it will take two of you to work on piecing your relationship back together.

Although many people not only suggest, but also encourage a period of separation, I do not believe a marriage can be saved by being apart. That isn't to say it won't ever work, but rather that in my experience trial separations do not result in reconciliation. Now, when I talk about separation I'm referring to a couple actually living apart, not just spending a few days away from each other. While exceptions to my theory certainly do exist, my rule is this: *If you want to stay married, don't separate*. Think about it. The reason you are contemplating divorce in the first place is because things are occurring in your marriage that you don't like. How in the world can you fix any issues when you are apart if you find it impossible to work on them when you are together?

If you reach a point in which both parties are committed to trying to save the marriage it is imperative that you seek help from the outside and resist the temptation of turning to a friend or family member. Why? Because at this difficult time you need someone who isn't part of the baggage of your past, can look at your situation objectively, and can offer solutions without being emotional. I don't care if you confide in your spiritual leader or choose a licensed mental health professional so long as he or she is a properly trained and totally unbiased third party.

It is also essential that you remember to give your spouse some breathing room. Constantly hovering or incessantly talking about your relationship will not help. It amazes me that high school or college behavior often continues into marriage. Remember when you considered breaking up with the person you were dating, but weren't one hundred percent certain if you should? What happened? Despite telling your boyfriend or girlfriend that you needed a little space, he or she called you constantly, asking what was wrong or wanting to get together. As a result, even though you initially really just needed some space, you ultimately decided the relationship was too much and so you ended it.

As surprising as it might seem, things don't change a whole lot when people get married. I can't tell you how often I see the person contemplating divorce agree to work on the marriage only to proceed with the divorce anyway because the other spouse wouldn't leave him or her alone. Believe it or not, the multiple *I love you* texts and emails are often looked at as a form of harassment rather than endearment.

You need to try and be realistic. The grass isn't always greener on the other side, it's just different, and Groundhog Day occurs more often than once a year on February 2nd. Most relationships go through a period of time when it feels like every single day is exactly the same. This is when renewing a "friendship" with a high school boyfriend or girlfriend can be particularly dangerous. If you removed all the fattening food from your house in an effort to lose weight, would you hang out at a donut shop? Not if you wanted to stay on your diet. Correspondingly, if you are married with kids, a mortgage, a job, and a spouse who you feel like is always complaining, you shouldn't be reviving a relationship you had when your parents took care of your living expenses, and the only person you had to worry about was yourself.

Working to save your marriage is an incredibly tough process. However, you must ask yourself this question: "In five or ten years time will I look back and regret not trying?" When you consider this make sure you are thinking about yourself, and not just your children. It is amazing how often clients will claim they are staying married for the sake of the kids. I call them on this every time. If you are that unhappy, what kind of role model are you? In reality, you are showing your children what an unloving, uncommunicative, and contentious relationship is all about. Do you really want your children to follow in your footsteps?

What has surprised me the most since I started practicing family law is that children of majority age often have a harder time dealing with their parents' divorce than younger children. Older children tend to start questioning the reality of their youth, and whether their whole life was a lie. I can only assume that the parents who stayed together for the sake of their children didn't see that one coming.

This takes me back to *you*, and not having any regrets. There is quite a difference between going through a very difficult time—even if it seems never-ending—and truly being unhappy. Coming to terms with where you are is the most challenging part. However, not giving yourself time may be the difference between having regrets for the rest of your life or not.

Chapter Three

WHAT SHOULD I DO NOW?

So, either you or your spouse has decided to take that big step toward divorce. What do you do now? The first thing you need to do is check your emotions at the door, and DON'T BURN THE UNDERWEAR!

Emotional reactions are rarely, if ever, the best reactions. When a client of mine discovered his wife was having an affair, he proceeded to burn all her lingerie on the barbecue grill. However, by the time the ashes had cooled, he felt so guilty he bought her a brand new collection of bras and panties from Victoria's Secret.

When he called me to relate what he did, my immediate response was, "Well, that was stupid—now she has a brand new set of underwear for her boyfriend!"

While ninety percent of the cost of divorce is associated with emotions, only ten percent is related to the facts. In the end, it is that all-important ten percent that really matters. Trust me, I know it is easier said than done, but you will be better off both financially and emotionally if you make a conscious effort to work on controlling those emotions. Recognizing the difference between an emotional reaction and fact can be a challenging feat; however, understanding the difference is an essential element when going through a divorce.

The first emotion people are usually faced with when contemplating divorce is embarrassment. It doesn't matter if it is the person who wants the divorce, or the person upon whom the divorce is being thrust; both parties will feel embarrassed because they are convinced they have failed.

Embarrassment and a sense of failure are both guaranteed to catapult reactions that are based on pure unadulterated emotion. Getting divorced is not a failure, but rather is a sign that the relationship has come to an end. How often do you see best friends stop being friends? Do you see them as failures? Of course not. So why in the world when fifty percent of marriages end in divorce do people correlate their divorce with failure and embarrassment? It's because they are allowing their emotions to control their responses, which if not corrected, will greatly impact their divorce.

Acknowledging your feelings—and confronting them—is essential, and if you can't get past those feelings on your own you should absolutely speak with a counselor. Think about this, the hourly rate of a counselor is generally substantially less than the hourly rate of an attorney, is probably covered by insurance, and will directly address your feelings.

.   Let me illustrate. You have just been informed that your spouse wants a divorce, and although he or she denies having an affair, you believe this is far from the truth. As you experience a thousand emotions that range from anger, hurt, humiliation, stupidity, and embarrassment, you find yourself wanting to seek revenge. Your attorney tells you that although proof of an affair will have absolutely zero bearing on the outcome of your divorce, you have the right to look for evidence of the affair. This is your fork in the road. You can spend thousands of dollars on an attorney—and I am not kidding when I say thousands—trying to gather information on an alleged affair that won't make one iota of difference in your divorce case, or you can start counseling immediately and start addressing the real issue – your feelings and how the affair and breakdown of your marriage really affected you.

What's really interesting is that when my clients finally deal with their emotions and accept the breakdown of their marriage, they often realize that *they* weren't very happy either. Too many people go through life wearing blindfolds, and are genuinely shocked when the blindfolds are taken off. I have had numerous people share that they haven't had sex for five, ten, or even fifteen years, and still can't believe their spouse had an affair. If you had to place a bet on who could help these people the most, would you put your money on an attorney or a counselor?

If dealing with your emotions wasn't enough, you will need to consult with an attorney. Finding an attorney is easy. Just go online. However, finding an attorney who is qualified to handle your particular divorce may be another story. It's guaranteed that you'll get plenty of recommendations from family and friends, and while this is an excellent way to acquire the name of an attorney, this method should never be seen as the sole prerequisite. Although some referrals may be spot-on, others will resemble the telephone game where "a friend tells a friend who tells a friend."

I'll never forget the call I received from a potential client who had been told I was "the absolute best attorney" because I got a former client custody of his stepchild. While it is always nice to receive accolades such as this, being the absolute best attorney also requires full disclosure. I explained that although my former client did receive custody of his children, he did not get, nor did we request, legal custody of his stepchild. My point is that a referral is merely a recommendation, which may or may not be based on fact, and is why you must do your own thorough research.

The Internet is by far the easiest research tool to use. Check out websites such as www.lawyers.com, www.Martindale.com, www.superlawyers.com, and www.AAML.org (American Academy of Matrimonial Lawyers). Find out if the attorney you are thinking of retaining even lists divorce, domestic law, or family law as an area in which he or she practices. If the attorney doesn't even acknowledge practicing in one of these areas, you need to think twice. The above websites will also provide you with information regarding how an attorney's peers rate his or her ethical standards and professional abilities. However, don't forget that even though the information provided on these websites is helpful, it is still only a tool to help you learn more about the attorney you are considering retaining.

The next and most important step is to meet with your chosen attorney. This initial meeting is generally referred to as a consultation, and while some attorneys may offer a free consultation at this stage, most will charge their hourly rate, which will vary depending on the state and county in which you reside.

People are often surprised when they learn that attorneys charge for consultations. However, they shouldn't be surprised for a number of reasons. First of all, when you are consulting with an attorney, you are asking him or her to give you legal advice based on education and experience for which the attorney had to pay. Secondly, if you can't afford to pay for an initial consultation with an attorney, you probably can't afford to retain that attorney to handle your entire divorce.

Once you have the name of an experienced divorce attorney you can afford, it's time to schedule a consultation. Although I could offer you a list of excellent questions to ask during the initial consultation, the reality is that you probably won't remember much. This is why you may want to consider having a friend or family member accompany you. However, if you choose this route, you must be aware that you will not be protected by the attorney-client privilege. The significance of the attorney-client privilege is something you should discuss with the attorney, and should be weighed against the need for you to have support and another set of ears during the meeting.

Although the initial consultation is very important, what you need to take away from it is pretty basic – you have to be comfortable and be able to communicate with the person who is going to represent you in the divorce. There is nothing easy about getting divorced, and the divorce process will only be that much more difficult if you aren't comfortable with or have trouble communicating with your attorney I don't care that the person who referred you said that the attorney you are meeting with is the best in the city; even if that attorney has a plaque stating that exact thing, do not hire that attorney.

Part of being comfortable is being aware of how the attorney communicates with you and the opposing counsel. While letters or emails may be the primary form of communication, you need to know if the attorney will pick up the phone. There are times in every case when letters or emails are misinterpreted because the tone becomes that of the recipient as opposed to its author. **If you retain an attorney who will not use the phone to answer a question or verify any information received, you can fully expect your divorce to cost more and take longer than necessary.** Additionally, it is essential to determine an attorney's policy when it comes to responding to emails and voicemails. Although a twenty-four hour, or even a forty-eight hour response time is reasonable, not hearing back for over a week is unacceptable.

It is not uncommon for a senior attorney to meet with a client initially and then have a younger attorney do the majority of the work As long as you understand and agree with this arrangement, there is nothing wrong with it. However, if you find out after you retain the attorney with whom you met that a younger attorney has actually been assigned your case, you could find yourself being represented by someone you don't feel is competent. That is why you need to make certain that you are told during the consultation which attorney will be handling your case on a day-to-day basis.

Assuming your research has already confirmed that your chosen attorney is qualified to handle your divorce, you shouldn't spend much time, if any, discussing the attorney's experience. Rather, you should find out how frequently the attorney handles cases in the county in which your divorce will be filed. Normally there are local rules for each county as well as state laws. Local rules establish practices and procedures that are unique to each county. In addition, there are often guidelines that have been created and are followed by attorneys and judges. While these guidelines are not "rules" that judges are mandated to consider, they do offer an indication of what the court will do. If the attorney you are meeting with does not regularly practice in that county, it is unlikely that he or she will be familiar with the local rules, guidelines, and even more importantly, the judge assigned your case. Is this really the person you want representing you?

However, as I keep saying, there are always exceptions. If you meet with an attorney with whom you really click, but who unfortunately doesn't normally practice in the county in which your divorce will be filed, you could still hire him or her along with "local counsel." Local counsel is an attorney who regularly practices in your county and can offer your selected attorney assistance with local practices and procedures. Having two attorneys will obviously cost you more, but that doesn't mean you have to pay double the fees. Local counsel's role can be limited to keeping the other attorney apprised of the local rules and appearing in court with him or her—if that is all you want. **Remember, this is your ship, and you are the captain.** Although you might be unfamiliar with the waters, you really do get to decide the direction of the ship.

While it is essential that you convey your expectations to your attorney, he or she must let you know if those expectations are reasonable. One of the most difficult things an attorney may have to tell you is that you aren't being realistic, or that your expectations aren't in your best interest. Although I can pretty much guarantee you won't always like what you hear, you will thank your attorney for telling you the truth in the end.

One of the most frequent questions I am asked during initial consultations is whether the parent with whom I am meeting will get "full" custody of his or her children. The problem with this question is that there really isn't such a thing as "full" custody. You need to think of custody more in terms of an outline with part one being Roman numeral I and part two being Roman numeral II. Roman numeral I is referred to as legal custody. Legal custody is what gives a party the right to make decisions about a child's education, religion, medical care, and overall general welfare. In a divorce proceeding a parent can request either sole or joint legal custody. As you would expect, sole custody means that only one parent makes decisions regarding the child, whereas joint legal custody provides equal decision-making authority. The second part of the outline, or Roman numeral II, is what is generally referred to as physical or residential custody, and controls where a child will reside.

What is essential to understand is that the preference of the courts in most states is to grant parents joint legal custody, and to implement a schedule that gives each parent specific days and times with the children. This is often referred to as "Parenting Time or a Visitation Schedule." That is not to say that a court will never award sole legal custody, but rather that it is rare. It is rare because unless a parent poses an identifiable risk to a child, or there is an exceptionally unusual situation, the courts recognize more than ever that children need both parents in their lives. It is important to understand that even if you were awarded sole legal custody, your spouse is still going to receive parenting time with his or her children, except in extreme circumstances.

Let's circle back to the consultation and having realistic expectations. For the sake of argument, imagine you are a stay-at-home mother, and your soon-to-be-ex-husband (or what I recently heard referred to as a "wasband") is a workaholic who has never changed a diaper, taken the children to the doctor, attended a parent/teacher conference, or stayed alone with the children overnight. Assuming you live in a state where the preference is joint legal custody, the attorney should tell you straight up that the likelihood you will receive sole legal custody based on those facts alone is slim-to-none. In fact, depending on the state in which you live, the attorney may inform you that requesting sole legal custody for the reasons you presented could actually hurt you, because one of the factors a court considers is which parent is most likely to foster a relationship with the other parent. In this example, the father could argue that the request for sole legal custody exemplifies the mother's attempts to alienate him and damage the relationship he hopes to maintain with his children.

Imagine how you would feel if the attorney you hired failed to explain the preference for joint legal custody, or how requesting sole custody could be used against you. Here's the bottom line: if your attorney offers you a reasonable explanation as to why your request is either unrealistic or not in your best interest, you should take the advice seriously. Remember, you hired your attorney based on his or her experience.

Something else you need to consider in your consultation is whether the attorney is trying to calm you down or ignite the fire. Sometimes the emotional response during a divorce is the attorney's and not the client's. It is not unusual for me to explain to a client that a detailed tit-for-tat response isn't necessary, especially if it has nothing to do with the case. On an almost a daily basis I have to warn clients that the letter, email, or formal document I am about to forward will inevitably upset them, but that they must try their best to concentrate on the real issues, rise above any emotionally-charged statements, and ignore the garbage.

Unfortunately, it's not unusual for a person representing himself, or even an attorney, to forward letters or file documents with the court that contain inflammatory and inaccurate statements. Such was the situation when an opposing party filed a fifteen-page motion that was replete with falsehoods. Instead of immediately firing back a response to put the "record" straight, I filed a concise direct response. As a result, my client did not incur the cost for me to file an extensive response, and the judge denied the motion without a hearing. At times like this, it is important to take a deep breath and ensure that your reaction—and your attorney's—is not weighed with emotion, but well thought-out.

If your attorney responds to situations emotionally, or continually fuels your fire, you need to take control of your ship and talk to your attorney about changing course. If you don't, the financial and emotional cost of your divorce case can escalate faster than you can blink an eye.

Chapter Four

WHO SHOULD I LISTEN TO, AND WHAT IF I CAN'T AFFORD AN ATTORNEY?

When you start down the path of divorce it is only a matter of time before the news will spread to family, friends, neighbors, and people you don't even know. Sharing intimate details, they will tell you what they had to endure during their divorce and how they are still suffering the consequences. Everyone will have a piece of advice for you because if they haven't been through a horrible divorce themselves, they will definitely know someone who has been. They may even tell you about their best friend's uncle's son from Alaska who went through the divorce from hell.

When people share these stories, you must remember that they genuinely believe they are helping. However, the best thing you can do is ignore everything they say. Even if they were divorced in the same state and county where yours is currently filed, you must realize that every divorce is unique. No case or judge is exactly alike, and even if you happen to have the same judge, judges are people too; and what may impact that judge's decision one day may not make a difference the next.

Although it would be nice to believe that you will now be able to completely ignore other peoples' suggestions, the reality is that you are bound to listen to at least one golden nugget of advice that will leave you wondering why your attorney did this, or didn't do that. How do I know? Because despite warning my clients, I still get calls that go something like this:

"I know you advised me not to listen to other people, and I've been doing a really good job, but someone just said I'll get a large lump sum of maintenance (otherwise known as alimony) because I've been married for over ten years. Is that true?"

The short answer to this question was *no*. The longer answer that was necessary for my client to feel comfortable included a reminder of the factors that a court considers when a party is requesting maintenance. While I wished that what she had heard was correct, the parties' incomes and assets were minimal at best, which meant that when she reached the end of her divorce, she would not find a pot of gold.

I know how difficult it is to ignore well-meaning advice, but unless you want to go out of your mind, **stop listening to other people. Listen to the person you are paying and *trust* – your attorney!**

What happens if you can't afford an attorney? Well, you need to recognize the difference between retaining an attorney and consulting with one. While I completely understand that you may not have the means to retain an attorney to handle your case from start to finish, you should make every attempt to at least consult with one.

During a consultation, an attorney can provide you with information on the laws in the state in which you live and also make you aware of your county's local rules. Additionally, you will learn how courts generally decide issues, and how your specific case may be similar or dissimilar to the average case. The attorney should also be able to tell you if your state has self-help forms that you could complete yourself, and if it would make sense in your case. Let me be clear, state self-help forms are not forms you buy on-line from "xyz company" or from your local office supply store. They are forms that are approved by the state, and frequently can be found on-line at your state's judicial website.

It is important to remember that consulting with an attorney does not obligate you to retain that attorney to represent you. However, you need to keep in mind what could be at stake if you don't hire an attorney. Are you fighting over your children? Do you have substantial assets that need to be divided, such as real estate, a business, retirement, or investments? If so, you should seriously consider retaining an attorney. Alternatively, if there isn't a dispute regarding children or if your assets are minimal, the self-help forms and one or two consultations with an attorney may be sufficient. You need to try and look at your case as objectively as possible, because the last thing that you should be doing is paying an attorney thousands of dollars to solely fight over who is going to take more debt. Again, this is something you should discuss during your consultation, because in the end, it's all about making the best long-term decision for *you*.

Chapter Five

WHAT INFORMATION IS IMPORTANT, AND HOW AND WHEN SHOULD I GET IT?

The information you will need for your divorce is directly related to what is at issue. In other words, if child or spousal support is going to be an issue, the income of both parties will be classed as important information. Likewise, if assets and debts are to be divided, it is essential that you have a detailed accounting of all of your assets and debts.

As I will soon explain, don't worry if you don't have any information regarding your financial situation, because you should be able to obtain what you need during the divorce process. If you happen to be someone who has no idea how much your spouse makes, or what the marital estate is worth, there is no reason to shut down or be embarrassed. Believe it or not, you are far from being alone, as this is not an unusual situation. It's amazing how many spouses are deliberately kept in the dark.

There are actually wives who are told to sign joint tax returns while their husbands cover the front page with their hand. Although it is easy to become accustomed to doing this and think nothing of it at the time, in hindsight, there is obviously something seriously wrong with this picture.

So, when should you gather the information you need, and how should you get it? The answers are simple—the sooner the better, and the best way you can. Obtaining copies of the last five years of tax returns is a great place to start. If you know where your tax returns are kept, and have access to them, make copies immediately. Even if you are uncertain whether you want to go ahead with the divorce, this is always good information to possess. If you don't have access to the tax returns, and you file jointly, you have every right to obtain copies from your accountant (even if your spouse covered the front page as you signed them). However, it's important to be aware that your accountant may tell your spouse what you asked for, which depending on your situation, may not be what you want. As an alternative, if you aren't comfortable asking your accountant, you could request copies from the IRS, but don't forget to think about who picks up the mail

Correspondence, no matter what it is, could be intercepted by your spouse.

In the event your spouse has either told you a divorce is imminent, or has actually started divorce proceedings, *nothing* should deter you from asking your accountant or the IRS for copies of your tax returns, including your inner demons. Once you have the returns in hand, you must put them in a safe place. If you have an attorney, then his or her office is obviously your "safe" place. Otherwise, I suggest you store the copies at work, in a safe deposit box, or with family or friends. However, whatever you do, do not keep them in your car. Why? Because your spouse probably has the second car key! Although this may seem obvious to someone who isn't involved in a divorce, I have had to advise at least fifty percent of my clients not to choose this hiding place.

In addition to tax returns, you should collect copies of any document that provides evidence of your and your spouse's incomes, assets, and debts over the last three to five years. The type of documents I am referring to include bank statements, investment accounts, retirement accounts, life insurance policies, credit cards, appraisals, and mortgages. However, remember that these are just examples of the documents you might need. In reality, you can never have too much information, but it is possible to have too little. Think hard about your personal situation, and what might be important in your case.

During your consultation with the attorney, be sure to ask if the courts treat inherited or gifted property differently than property that was jointly acquired during your marriage. If there is a difference, you should gather any documentation that verifies the value of the property at the time of your marriage. For example, if you had a retirement account when you married, try and locate the document that shows the value of the account at that time.

The only exception to this rule relates to your household goods and furnishings. Unless your household goods and furnishings are collectible items that are worth a substantial amount of money, nobody will care what value you place on them. Why? Because no one cares who gets them in the end. Trust me, if you and your spouse start arguing over the silverware, breakfast table or Tupperware in court, not only will everyone become frustrated, including the judge, but you will also spend far more money in attorney's fees than the items are actually worth.

If you are unable to collect all the documents you need for your divorce, or your spouse refuses to provide the documents voluntarily, the discovery process will help you obtain them. This could involve asking your spouse to produce the documents, or request that he or she grant you access to any financial accounts online. This type of discovery is referred to as a Request for Production of Documents, and should allow you to procure copies of documents such as tax returns, bank statements, copies of bookkeeping programs like Quicken, and credit card statements.

There is also another form of discovery known as Interrogatories, which involves questions that have been reduced to writing, and have to be answered within a specified period of time The good thing about Interrogatories is that the questions must be answered under oath, and if the answers provided aren't truthful, they could potentially be used against your spouse in the future. The bad thing about Interrogatories is that the answers are generally crafted with the assistance of an attorney, which can result in the spouse technically answering the question, but avoid supplying the answer the other spouse really wanted.

For example, say your soon-to-be-ex purchased gifts for an alleged girlfriend, and he is asked to specify what he bought, when he bought it, and how much he paid. He could claim that he purchased a pair of earrings that cost him less than $100, and that he may have purchased other gifts, but he can't recall if he did or didn't at this time. While his response is obviously not the answer you wanted, in the world of litigation, it is still an answer. With that being said, it doesn't mean you don't have any recourse. If you and your attorney believe it is appropriate to try and compel your spouse to in effect change his or her answer, you can engage the court by filing a motion requesting that the court order the Interrogatory to be supplemented with a response that is complete and not evasive.

If you find yourself in this situation, it is extremely important to communicate with your attorney and discuss whether you just disliked the answer because you found it vague and annoying, or if the answer was truly unresponsive to the discovery request. It is essential that you weigh the attorney fees that will be incurred to "prove" your spouse was untruthful against the real value of the information you seek. In other words, how much money are you willing to spend to simply unearth evidence that your spouse had an affair? Especially if the fact that he or she was unfaithful will have no bearing whatsoever on the final outcome of your divorce. In comparison, if your spouse refuses to disclose his income by failing to provide you with bank statements, how much money are you willing to spend to obtain *that* evidence?

This section is not meant to provide you with a detailed explanation of the discovery process, but rather to offer a basic explanation and present examples of the ways in which you can obtain information and documents from "the other side."

There are numerous discovery tools to assist you during your divorce, including requiring your spouse to appear at your attorney's office and to verbally respond to questions at the time they are asked. This is called a deposition, and while this is a very effective method of getting "real time" answers, it can also be very expensive. You not only incur the cost for your attorney to prepare for and take the deposition, but also the cost of the court reporter and transcript.

Prior to engaging in a full-blown discovery attack**, it is essential that you fully understand what you are looking for, why you are looking for it, and if it will make a difference in your divorce.** You also need to determine if you already have access to the information. If you don't have access, you should find out if you can obtain it voluntarily to avoid having to issue costly methods of formal discovery.

What makes me crazy is when an opposing attorney racks up fees by issuing formal discovery when it isn't necessary. **While it is true the attorney is the expert, there is nothing wrong with clients asking if a specific action will be of benefit to them, and if so, if it can be done less expensively.**

I will never forget an instance when a client and I were about to meet with the opposing party and her counsel to discuss temporary issues. My client arrived early to tell me that he and his wife had already met with their financial advisor who had prepared a balance sheet that detailed all of their assets and debts and proposed an equal division of all of the accounts.

When my client's wife and her attorney showed up at my office, I immediately brought up the great news about the parties' meeting with their financial advisor and suggested that we bypass discussions regarding temporary issues and concentrate on the final division of assets and debts. Unfortunately, my opposing counsel was not on the same page. In fact, she wasn't even in the same book. She immediately stood up and started flailing her arms. "We can't do that," she yelled. "I need to send out formal discovery!"

Now remember, this was a case in which the clients met with their financial advisor jointly, and they were both in possession of exactly the same information regarding their incomes, assets, and debts. It was neither a situation in which one of the clients was completely uninformed about their financial situation, nor was it a situation in which one of the clients suspected there were hidden assets, or that assets had been dissipated.

After the opposing counsel's outburst, my client asked his soon-to-be-ex to, "Do something!"

Appearing completely shell-shocked, the wife did absolutely nothing, and just shrugged her shoulders. As a result, the wife's attorney sent out formal discovery and both parties ended up spending thousands more in attorney's fees.

Eventually, the wife hired a new attorney, and the case was finally settled using the original spreadsheet prepared by the parties' financial advisor. A story such as this serves to emphasize how you must continually remind yourself that you are the captain of your ship. While you will undoubtedly depend on your attorney—your first mate—you must maintain control of the ship's helm. If you are afraid or intimidated by your attorney, you either need to learn to speak up or get a new attorney.

As I tell my clients and opposing parties, you can pay for your children to go to college, or you can pay for mine to go to college. It's up to the two of you.

Chapter Six

WHAT WILL HAPPEN DURING THE DIVORCE PROCESS, AND HOW MUCH WILL IT COST?

Courts recognize the commencement of an action for divorce by the filing of a Petition (or Complaint), frequently referred to as a Petition for Divorce, Petition for Dissolution of Marriage or Divorce Complaint.

Once the Petition is filed, the way in which you choose to notify your spouse will determine the initial path of your divorce. Assuming this wasn't a joint decision, there is a good chance your spouse will be very surprised. However, it doesn't have to happen like it does in the movies. You don't have to have someone hand your spouse the Petition and announce, "You've been served!"

To minimize the impact, you can provide your spouse with a copy of the Petition and a document to sign that acknowledges he or she has received it. There is an inherent difference between being offered the choice of accepting a Petition and being subjected to the uncomfortable and often embarrassing act of being served. While I do not profess to have a degree in the field of mental health, it doesn't take a rocket scientist to understand that having the choice to voluntarily accept something feels better than having it forced upon you.

There are of course exceptions when having a Petition formally served is your only choice. You should definitely choose this option if there is a history of domestic violence or if you are genuinely concerned filing for divorce will provoke a violent reaction.

While formal service involves an independent third party delivering the Petition to your spouse and then verifying the time and place of service, it doesn't mean you have to rely on the Sheriff. You can use a process server, who is just a man or woman in regular clothing. In addition to choosing who delivers the Petition, you can also choose where and when your spouse is served

Although a statement such as, "After what she did to me, you're darn right I want to embarrass her at work," illustrates a typical emotional reaction, you need to be careful what you ask for. If you start the divorce based on revenge, have no doubt that your soon-to-be-ex will feel completely justified in his or her retaliation.

Once the Petition has been "served," a response or answer will need to be filed. Additionally, you may need to address issues such as temporary support, which of the parties will continue to reside in the marital residence, and where the children will live during divorce proceedings. At this point, you will once again find that the direction of your divorce is completely up to you and your spouse. If you refuse to communicate directly, and go through your attorneys instead, there will be a delay in the exchange of information, and the cost of your divorce will only increase.

Similarly, the number of times you appear in court is directly related to how often you and your spouse disagree. When it comes to issues in your divorce, you can either reach a mutual decision, or let the court decide for you. In some states, as long as you are represented by an attorney, and have settled every issue by agreement, you might never have to set foot in a courtroom. Conversely, in few states you could actually have a jury trial, and submit certain issues of your divorce case to a "jury of your peers."

If a case does go to trial, the process involves an enormous amount of preparation and expense. The attorney has to prepare an opening statement to tell the judge or jury about the case, and a closing statement to sum it up. He or she will have to prepare questions to ask you, your spouse, and anyone else testifying on your or your spouse's behalf. Your attorney also has to gather all the documents and exhibits that will be offered into evidence to support your position, and prepare you and your witnesses to testify

It is important that I keep reminding you that the cost associated with a divorce is not just financial, but emotional as well. **If you allow your emotions to take control, you can fully expect to have a long and arduous divorce.** I hope you understand that I am urging you to make decisions in your divorce as you would in business. Imagine you owned a retail store. If a customer started yelling and berating you, how would you react? Engaging in a confrontation with him or her would be a very bad business decision. To diffuse a situation, it's best to remain cool, calm, and collected, and to put your emotions to one side.

If your spouse starts verbally attacking you, step back and think about the repercussions of responding. If you tell him or her that you don't have to listen (which, by the way you don't), and remove yourself from the situation, you have not only gained control, but also saved yourself hundreds of dollars in attorney's fees. If you do retaliate, I can pretty much guarantee that one or both of you will contact your attorney and then the Battle of the Letters or the Filing of Motions Crusade will begin.

It is inevitable that after I have explained the state laws during a consultation, the person with whom I am meeting will say: "Well, that doesn't sound too bad. We should get this divorce over and done with really fast." My response is always that if the spouses can work together and keep a check on their emotions, then that is correct. Unfortunately, despite trying their best to overcome their feelings, clients usually allow their emotions to re-emerge. I have been inundated with voicemails and emails asking me what kind of motion can be filed with the court to stop the other spouse from doing a series of horrible things or to make the other spouse do something. Although your initial reaction may be that something must be done, it is of the utmost importance that you discuss with your attorney the pros and cons of taking any action.

It always amazes me that people in a contentious divorce want to "leave it up to the judge or jury." Think about it. You are offering the judge or jury one hundred percent control of your life. In other words, you are relying on someone who doesn't know you, your spouse, or your kids to make decisions that will significantly affect your future. **If you have to appear in court, it's highly unlikely you'll engage in a direct conversation with the judge, and the concept that you will get to tell "your story" is a fallacy.** Your story will either be conveyed by your attorney, or by you, in a question-and-answer format. When your attorney asks you specific questions, you will provide the answers. However, if the opposing attorney doesn't like the way a particular question was asked, he or she can object, and if the judge deems the question inappropriate, guess what? You don't get to answer it. Even worse, a judge might decide some of your story is insignificant, and you won't be allowed to relate it at all.

Although some judges immediately start the trial at the designated time, others will first want to talk to the attorneys. I was involved in a case that both sides worked extremely hard to settle. Unfortunately, we ended up having to go to trial because there were approximately five issues on which the parties could not agree. Prior to the commencement of the trial, the judge announced he wanted to talk to the attorneys. He told the opposing counsel and me that he was very familiar with the facts of the case, and didn't want to hear any opening statements. All he wanted to hear was testimony on the major issue before deciding how he would handle the remaining four issues.

After listening to the testimony and reviewing the documents the husband and wife produced for the first issue, the judge strongly suggested that the attorneys summarize the remaining four issues. Now, when a judge strongly suggests something he is not necessarily saying that you are prohibited from testifying about an issue. However, if your attorney has been practicing long enough, he or she is going to know if a judge's "strong suggestion" equates to a prohibition or not. In this case, after conferring with our clients, both my opposing counsel and I agreed to proceed by statements of counsel, which meant that in the end, the parties were only able to tell the judge a minute part of their individual stories.

I fully expect you are thinking: "But this is America. I have the constitutionally-protected right to tell my story." Yeah, not so much.

Figuratively speaking, the judge is "God," unless and until you go to the Court of Appeals. The judge has a tremendous amount of discretion, and his or her orders won't be changed unless the Court of Appeals finds error in the orders.

The moral of this tale is that you never know what will happen if you "leave it up to the judge." Imagine the story of your marriage covering one sheet of paper. The judge will only hear the equivalent of the bottom corner quarter-inch of the piece of paper.

Alternatively, if you and your spouse manage to work out your disagreements, the terms on which you have agreed to settle will be based on the whole piece of paper. Ask yourself this question: If I had a choice, would I rather have a decision about the rest of my life based on the entire story of my marriage or a fragment?

If you can't settle your case through exchanges between yourselves or your attorneys, having a formal trial in front of a judge (or in those few states a jury) is not the only option. You could try using Alternative Dispute Resolution methods instead. Although each state will have its own rules related to such methods, the two most common forms are Mediation and Arbitration.

Mediation involves the spouses choosing an unbiased third party—normally an attorney or judge who is not hearing their case—to help them reach an agreement. They can also choose whether or not they want the attorney they have retained to be present during the mediation. One of the most important aspects of mediation is that all discussions and negotiations will remain confidential. The theory is that if the parties don't have to worry about their words being used against them, mediation will promote settlement. The mediator's job is not to "order" the spouses to do anything, but rather to help them reach an agreement based on the mediator's knowledge of the law and the jurisdiction in which the couple's case has been filed.

It is essential to know that an agreement reached in mediation is not enforceable until both spouses affirm their agreement in writing. In other words, they can tentatively reach an agreement in mediation and still have the option of changing their minds after having time to think about it, and/or having a discussion with their attorneys.

Arbitration, on the other hand, is more like an informal trial because witnesses can testify on behalf of either spouse and evidence can be offered to support a spouse's position. Similar to a case presented to a judge in court, there are rules to be followed in arbitration, and the decision to have attorneys present is optional. However, that's where the similarities end. Arbitration is a private proceeding that involves the spouses choosing the judge or arbitrator, agreeing on what "rules" will be followed, and deciding on the formality or informality of the process. Additionally, the date arbitration will take place is based on the spouses and arbitrator's schedule rather than on the court's.

As I have said before, there is absolutely nothing easy about getting divorced, but it's important to know you do have choices along the way that can substantially reduce both the financial and emotional impact of an extremely difficult situation.

Chapter Seven

WILL MY KIDS BE OKAY?

Whether or not your children will be okay is completely up to you and your spouse. If you put the emotional baggage from your marriage to one side and concentrate on what is best for your children, they should be fine. On the other hand, if you choose to make scathing remarks about your spouse and reward your children for acting in the same scornful/caustic/disparaging manner, the likelihood you'll create issues that will stay with them well into adulthood is pretty darn good. Suffice to say; infants and toddlers sense negative energy as much as teenagers do.

How can a parent profess to be sensitive to a child's feelings if he or she insists on either allowing or creating shameful scenes? I know of an instance where a child witnessed his mother screaming and hanging onto the car as his father tried to back out of the driveway, and have had many a case in which parents use religion as their chosen weapon. After accusing a spouse of having an affair, a parent might tell the children that in the eyes of the religion they practice, their father or mother has committed a grievous sin. Help me out here. If the parent were so devoutly religious, wouldn't he or she grant forgiveness, which is the very foundation of the faith that the parent is hiding behind?

Although I completely understand why couples might believe staying in a loveless marriage is in the best interests of their family, the reality is that children are far better off living in two happy homes rather than in one miserable home. Let me put this in perspective. The environment in your home has probably either been one of constant fighting or one of little-to-no communication. Neither elicits good role modeling for your children's future relationships. **Having to share your children and not see them every day may be a devastating thought, but a peaceful environment will be substantially better for their well-being.**

The phrase "out of the mouths of babes" was never more applicable than when a five-year-old had the following conversation with his mother:

"Mommy, is Daddy going to come back here and live?"

"No honey, I'm sorry, but he isn't."

"Oh, but I thought everything was better because you weren't having grown-up arguments anymore."

It is important to note that in the situation above the parents had not only stopped fighting in front their child, but had also resisted saying destructive things about each other. Be aware that if despite living apart, you continue to exchange hostile and cutting remarks in front of your children; the problems they have related to the divorce will not go away.

I can't tell you the number of times I have seen one parent truly distraught about a child spending time with the other parent. Whenever I witness this situation I promptly offer to loan out my two children for the weekend. Although I have never had anyone take me up on this offer, it does seem to make parents think twice about their concerns.

I have also adopted the phrase "court-ordered relaxation" to describe the period of time children are with the other parent, because I don't care who you are—even the very best parent needs a break.

When going through a divorce, some parents can't come to terms with the reality that today the courts recognize the importance of both parents being involved in their children's lives. The fact that one parent was completely in charge of taking care of the children during the marriage while the other spouse spent his or her life at work does not signify that the parent who worked is any less important to the children. Let's face it—during a marriage each parent assumes a certain role, whether it's providing financial support or being responsible for the children's doctor's appointments, taking part in school activities, or preparing meals. This doesn't mean your roles can't change. Quite frankly, you will find yourself playing many different roles after the divorce. Unfortunately, what many forget is that when they are conveying the evils of their soon-to-be-ex to their children, they are putting down anything about the child that is remotely like the other parent. It is bad enough that children are collateral damage to a divorce. Don't make it worse by making them feel bad about themselves.

Although it is often a natural reaction to want to tell your child why you are getting divorced, especially if there has been an affair, please don't do it. Before the divorce, you didn't engage your fourteen-year-old in a conversation about your sex life, so why in the world would you now relate the intimate details of your spouse's indiscretion? If you really want to do what is in your child's best interest, keep it to yourself. Trust me, if your spouse is truly that bad, your children will soon figure it out by themselves.

Sometimes issues arise when a parent claims a child's safety or general welfare is at risk. I can't tell you the number of times a parent alleges the other parent is an alcoholic because he or she has a drink or two. There is a huge difference between having a couple of drinks and blowing a .195 on a breathalyzer. The trouble is that people who misuse the procedures implemented to protect children have made it difficult for anyone who is dealing with a soon-to-be-ex that really does have a substance abuse problem. If a child gets a splinter in his or her foot when walking on the outside deck, or is fed fast food three times a week, the child is not being exposed to an unsafe or dangerous environment, (yes, people do really make these types of allegations). Likewise, unless there is a legitimate concern, calling the police to do a "welfare check" on a child is not in the child's best interest.

What people fail to realize is that even in situations when there is an identifiable, documented risk to the child, the courts rarely cut the offending parent out of the child's life. Instead, the courts will endeavor to protect that relationship while simultaneously ensuring the safety of the child. A common way in which a court can accomplish this goal is by requiring supervised visitation. Although this might not be an ideal environment, it does allow the parent and child to spend time together until it is ascertained that an unsupervised situation is appropriate.

You and your soon-to-be-ex must make every effort to bury the pain and hurt you caused each other. The parenting of your child during and after the divorce can have everlasting effects, so before you make any decisions about your children, I urge you to repeat this mantra: *What is in the best interests of the children?*

Chapter Eight

WILL I EVER BE HAPPY AGAIN?

A common emotion during a divorce is fear. People are sure to ask themselves: Will I be able to make it on my own? Will my children be okay? Will I ever be happy again? The answer to all three questions is a resounding YES!

Fear is a terrible thing. It can immobilize you. If you look at the above questions again, you will see that they are all based on the unknown. The trick is to realize that knowledge will eliminate much of that fear.

It might take some time, but you will eventually realize that avoidance not only increases your anxiety, but also prolongs the inevitable. During the initial stage of divorce proceedings, it's not unheard of for a client to avoid me, and although that seems odd since I was hired to help, it really does happen. In order to overcome your fear of the unknown, I encourage you to tackle your divorce head-on because avoiding your attorney will not make the divorce go away. If you never had anything to do with finances during your marriage and are now terrified you won't be able to support yourself or the children, don't bury your head in the sand. Skirting the situation will only make matters worse, but gathering the documentation that discloses your finances will leave you feeling both empowered and informed.

The philosophy is the same in regard to your happiness. The amount of energy required to dwell on regrets and rehash events is exhausting, and quite honestly, you'll be a drag to be around. **As I remind my clients, there is only one person in this world you can control—and that person is you.** You can't control what your soon to-be-ex did to you, or what he or she may do in the future. However, you can absolutely control how you react and how it all affects you. If you wallow in your divorce, you will have a tough time moving on.

Several years ago, I was sitting on a bench waiting to pick one of my children up from camp when a woman started telling another woman about her recent divorce. At the end of a lengthy explanation that detailed how horrible her ex-husband was, she said she had come to terms with the fact that she was forty years old and that her life was over. On hearing this, even I was depressed. Negativity breeds like a wildfire. If you are currently surrounding yourself with people who constantly complain about their lives, husbands, wives, or exes, join a new group or look for happier friends.

A divorce does not mean your life is over. It means you are starting a brand new chapter, whether you wanted to or not. Instead of mourning the marriage you wanted but didn't have, work towards improving your future.

From the time the divorce is final, I believe it takes about a year for the fog to lift. However, once that happens, ultimate happiness is truly within your reach.

You just need to allow it to happen!

ACKNOWLEDGEMENTS

I was raised by two amazing parents, and while I didn't always agree with them, there was never a question of their unconditional love and support. My mother passed away much too early, and I miss her every single day. However, I recognize that I am still luckier than most because I was able to have her in my life in the first place. My mother's passing had a profound effect on me, and made me realize without a doubt that life is much too short to be unhappy. Fortunately, my father, who has always been one of my anchors, is still a significant part of my life. His integrity and business aptitude have been my benchmark, and I am lucky to not only have him as my father, but also to call him my friend.

To acknowledge the love and support that I share with my husband almost minimizes the importance of our relationship. My husband is my champion and staunch supporter. He is my devil's advocate, my best friend and my forever.

I would be remiss in not thanking my second mother, Alana Seelig, for being my moral compass and the person who I call to find out if I can still eat what's in the refrigerator; and Denise Saper for being part of our family and keeping my father young.

Thank you to my friend Amy Loper, and my husband, for waiting for my book for twenty years and believing in me; Lisa Schad for her friendship and reminding me to write it; and Cynthia Caldwell, Dena Manzo and Candy Merrill for their encouragement and support.

Thank you to the Mayor of Starbucks, Joel Goldman, and Susan Epstein for sharing with me their insight; and to my editor and cover designer Carrie Kabak for her time, advice, and patience with my impatience.

Last but by no means least, thank you to my children, who I love with all my heart, and who are truly amazing people. As they grow up, I hope they embrace the concepts that you can only control yourself, and that if you don't ask the question, the answer is no.

A preeminent divorce and family law attorney, Susan Saper Galamba is experienced in the courtroom as well as trained in mediation and arbitration. Recognized as a Super Lawyer, she is active in her local family law bar organizations, is a Fellow of the American Academy of Matrimonial Lawyers, and has maintained the highest possible AV rating in Martindale Hubbell's peer review rating system.

www.ingramcontent.com/pod-product-compliance
Lightning Source LLC
Chambersburg PA
CBHW071541170526
45166CB00004B/1503